Little Dancers

Written by Eleana Norton
Illustrated by Scott Norton

Published in print and electronic formats
ISBN 978-1-7387631-0-8 (book)
ISBN 978-1-7387631-1-5 (electronic book)

Edited by Rachel Huckel (rachelhuckel.com)

Illustrated by Scott Norton

This book is published independently by Eleana Norton. For enquiries, email eleana.poetry@gmail.com.

May the words I share
Carry hope
Inspire joy
Soothe loneliness

And glorify my ever-faithful God.

CONTENTS

My great-grandmother used to say
That bleeding hearts
Look like little dancing girls
So her garden became a stage
Each time the wind sang
And I learned that the freest dancers
Are the ones with open hearts
The ballerinas that not-so-gracefully
Let sadness bleed out
And anger pour over
And passion soak through
There isn't a costume that will hide my wounds
Yet still I dance
As bleeding hearts do.

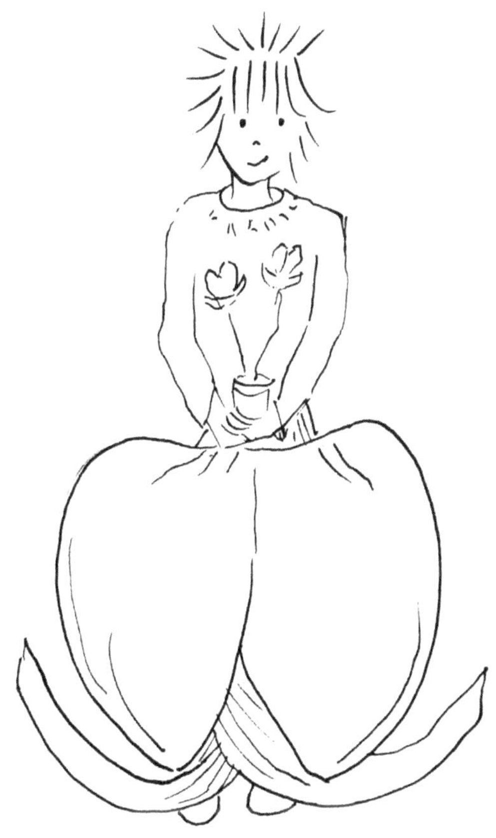

Waiting for Wings

I waited for wings
Like winter waits for the warmth of spring
Breathing in the fragrant hope
Exhaling with wordless wonder
As transformation reveals herself
Petal by petal
Feather by feather
Breath by breath
With joy on the horizon
Assurance rooted like birch trees
I waited for wings
That would carry me home.

All at once
I remember the hands of my childhood
And the strawberries they gathered
And the emptiness they filled

I remember
My grass-stained overalls
And my gold-stained gardens
And my red-stained baskets

I presented an offering
That the milkweed cradled
That the mourning doves nursed

It wasn't enough for you

All I have left
Are the bare fields of September
And the hollow hands of my childhood.

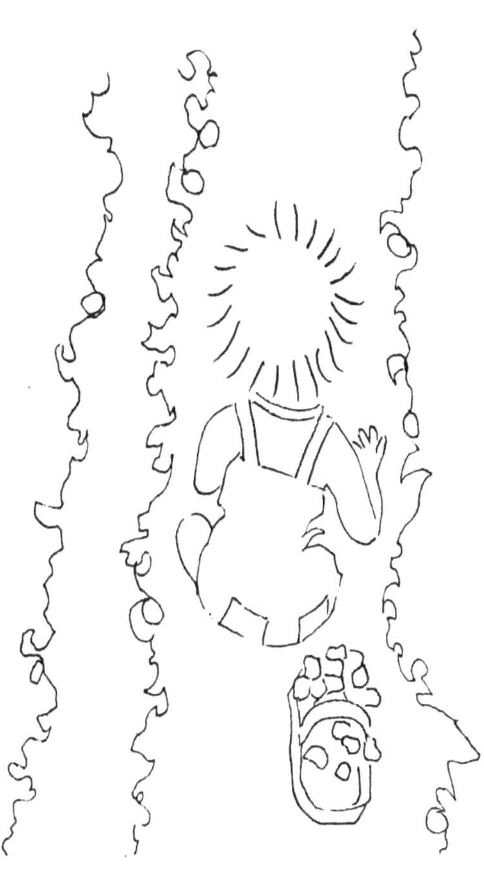

I was not a child
I was a lullaby
A song of surrender whispered
In delicate ears

I was not a girl in white pyjamas
I was a mother in a black dress
The weight of this loss in my arms
6 pounds 2 ounces

I was not a big sister
I was a chestnut tree
I would grow
I would blossom
And I would die every autumn

It isn't easy being a chestnut tree
Shoulders scorched by the sun
My ever-tired shoulders
My ever-empty arms.

A kindergarten performance
Dad watching in the front row
Today is a normal day

Family friend picks me up early
But I never leave school early
Today is a funny day

I ask questions in the car
She says she cannot answer
Today is a confusing day

Dad's face is puffy at the door
I've never seen him cry before
Today is an unusual day

Mom sitting on a corduroy couch
Holding a lifeless baby
Today is an empty day.

I was expecting skeletons
But I found hearts still beating
Love hanging from the rafters of childhood
Memories like dust
Resting on empty paintings
Six smiling faces
The image of misery
A black and white memory captured
And I wondered what you would see
In the newspapers we censored
In the chimneys we swept
In the attic.

I was four years old
When I learned how to carry a knapsack
And carry a loss
When people asked how many brothers I had
I learned not to count the ones in heaven
I learned you can't always be happy
For days off school
I learned a tree is planted
When a child dies
That prayers are answered
Though a mother cries
I learned about snow angels
And real ones named Doreen

I learned about love the day I learned about death.

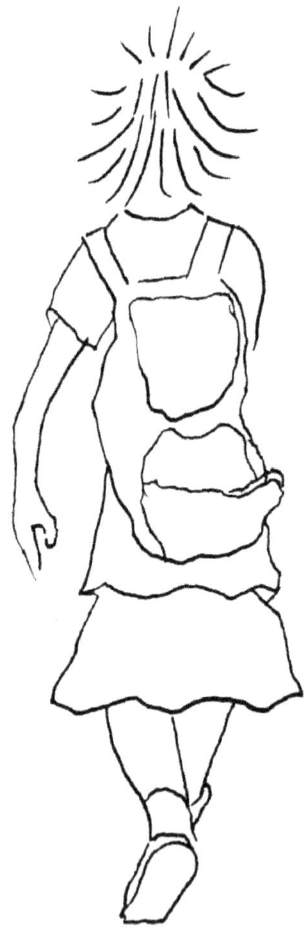

What good will come from this?

I can only hope
These tears will water a garden
This endless climb will make a way
And this emptiness will make room
For good to come from this.

When I don't listen
The birds still sing

Though I don't hear You now
I know You still speak

I see a crescent
Yet the moon is still round

Don't feel your presence
But still love abounds.

If I were a tree
I'd be the smallest sapling
Swayed by the softest winds
Tickled by the faintest dew
Who bows under the weight of a single raindrop
Who notices the arrival of the sun's first rays
If I were a tree
I would still be potted
As I wait for my roots to find a home
As I wait for my branches to brush the heavens
Still I am rising
Still I am growing.

Look up
Said the moon
Find hope for the night
Look up
Said the bird
Let wonder arise
Look up
Said the leaf
From the tallest tree
Look up
Said the wind
That twirled my hair
Look up said the staircase that swirled
The tomato plant that sprouted
And the cat that played on the roof
Look up said the bridges
The lamp posts
The churches
Look up said the smoke
The steam
The stars

Look up, said the heavens.

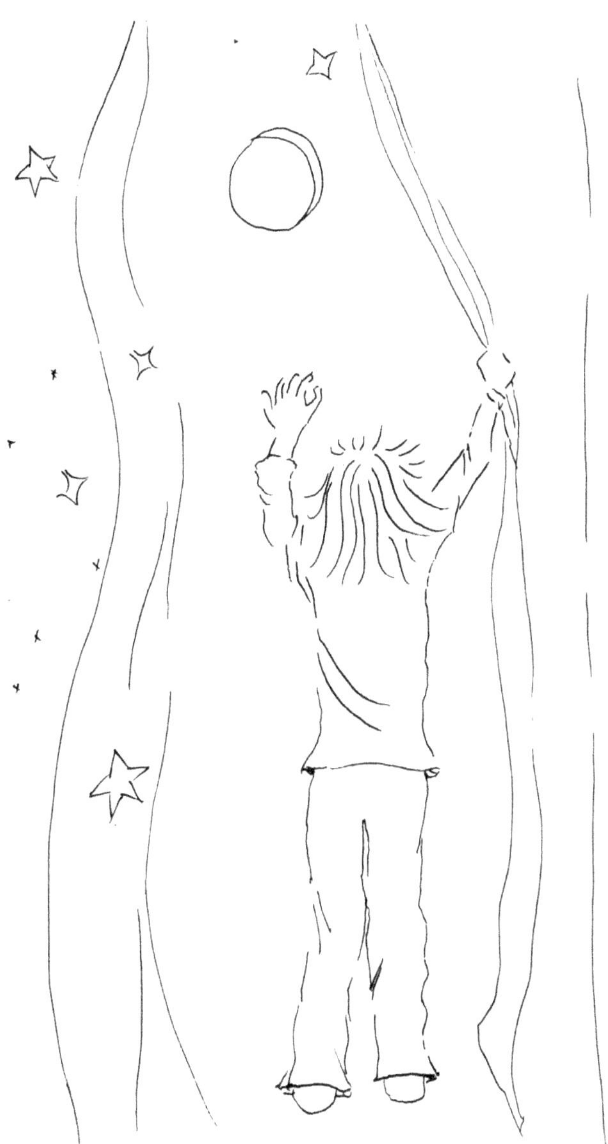

Little Blue Morpho
The world is not your foe
Open your wings
To the winds of serenity

Little Blue Morpho
Let days be ever slow
Open your wings
To the heart of simplicity

Little Blue Morpho
May you learn to let go
Open your wings
To the arms of divinity.

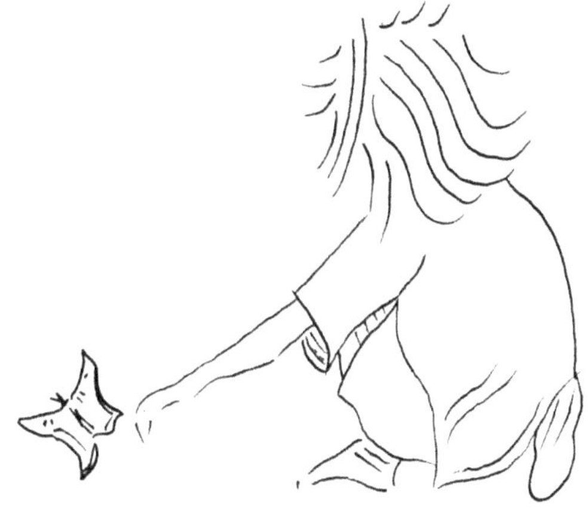

If Autumn was a poet
She'd write about hope
Braiding rhymes of golden rod and asters
Colouring the fields after summer blooms scatter

If Autumn was a musician
She'd sing songs of thanksgiving
Making melodies of crunchy leaves
And the delicate ones as they fall from trees

If Autumn was a mother
She'd be French Canadian
Serving you warm shepherd's pie
And sweet apple cider.

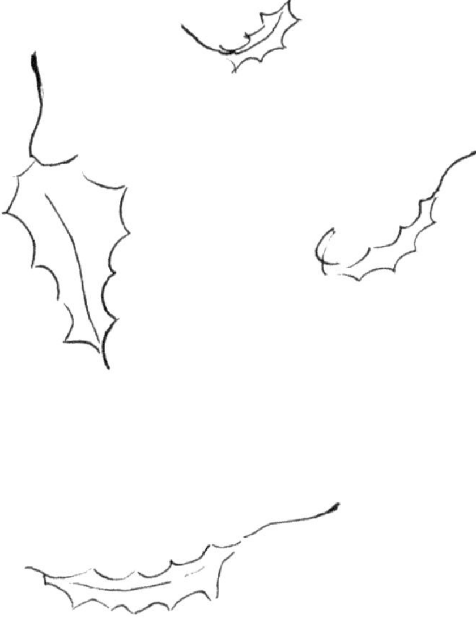

I never found safety in a place
But I found it in a person
Who yields strength with a song
Who forms home in His hands

Surely I am safe
Surely I am home
Surely I am His

For Jesus is
A warm embrace
Showers of grace
My peaceful space
My safest place.

I can still hear my grandpa's loving voice singing:
"Je sais qu'un jour, mes yeux verrons Jésus"

My brain didn't comprehend the words
But my heart remembered the melody
And my soul welcomed the peaceful tune
That can only be sung
By a man as sure of his eternity
As my papa was.

I hope my daughter knows joy
Like kitchen stand-up comedy
Like recycling box creativity
Like bath time karaoke

I hope she knows comfort
Like post-dinner art lessons
Like summer camp canoeing
Like thunderstorm blanket forts

I hope my daughter knows love
Like corduroy couch musicals
Like living room dance parties
Like Edelweiss harmonies

I hope my daughter knows a dad
Like mine.

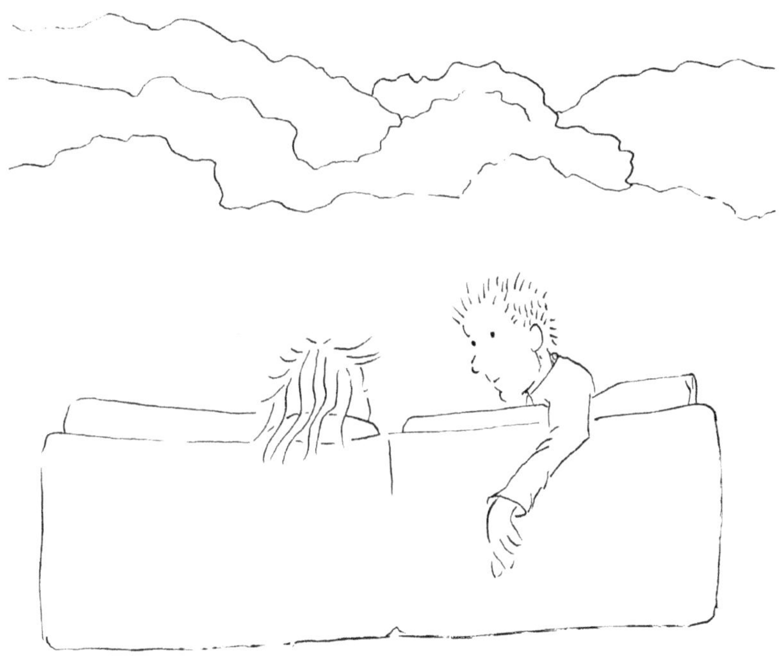

I watched a two-year-old twirl
Graceful as a maple key
I saw her jump as freely
As a seed that meets the wind
She stepped into my shadow
My unpointed toes
Imperfectly bent knees
And I saw
A head crowned in joy
A body robed in innocence
And I heard
A gentle whisper
The voice of my Father:
The way you see this daughter
Is the way I see you
O daughter of mine.

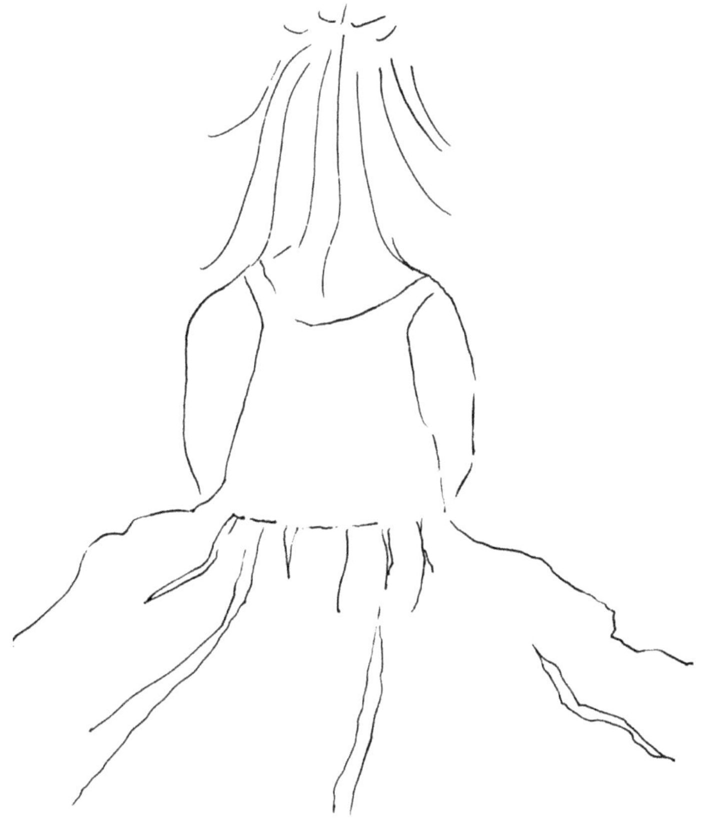

How do words become a poem?

Like caterpillar becomes butterfly
    Wondrously
Like yarn becomes sweater
    Patiently
Like apples become pie
    Lovingly
Like friend becomes stranger
    Painfully
Like girl becomes woman
    Beautifully.

If even you and I can hear the impact
Of a caterpillar falling from a tree

How much more does our Heavenly Father
Notice those who have yet to take flight?

I carry the memories of my childhood
As tightly as I held my helium-filled birthday balloon
Knowing that I can't get back what I let go

But I carry the memories of my twenties
With the open hands I use to hold a butterfly
Hoping she will have the courage to fly away.

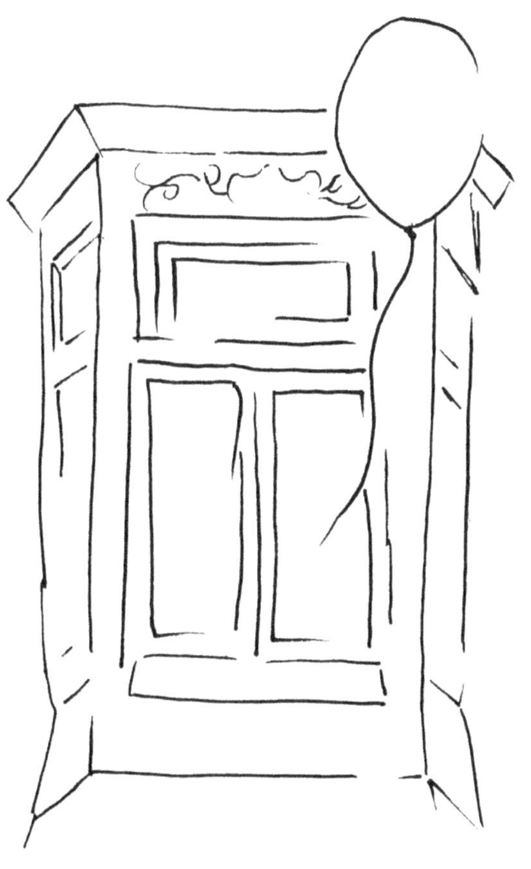

Under trembling leaves
The quivering of little faith
Doubts the wind's consistency
But I knew I wasn't alone
I found myself
Nestled in branches like perfect love
The kind that makes fear forget her name
I learned that
Butterfly wings
Carry the lightness of abandoned worries
And feel as strong as the wings of eagles.

Lonely Longings

Some days
There were effective placebos
And adequate distractions
So my eyes grew used to the darkness
And my stomach stopped hearing the growl
Other days
I was desperate for a cure
Petals turned
Curtains opened
Hands outstretched
I reached for every lightning bug
Thinking one would light my path
I wished on every dandelion
Forgetting flowers become weeds
That sneak into restless days
That poison dreamless nights
Until one day
I'm picking weeds that look like flowers
Longing for everything that looks like love.

The next day
I didn't notice the bruise
Chose to ignore the purples and blues
Casting a shadow that silently grew

I wore my best dress
Planted flowers I knew wouldn't bloom
Swallowed his guilt on a silver spoon
Proved to myself that life could resume

But two years later
I'm finding scars that turn into wounds
I'm entering tunnels I thought I'd been through
Still haunted by pain I tried to subdue.

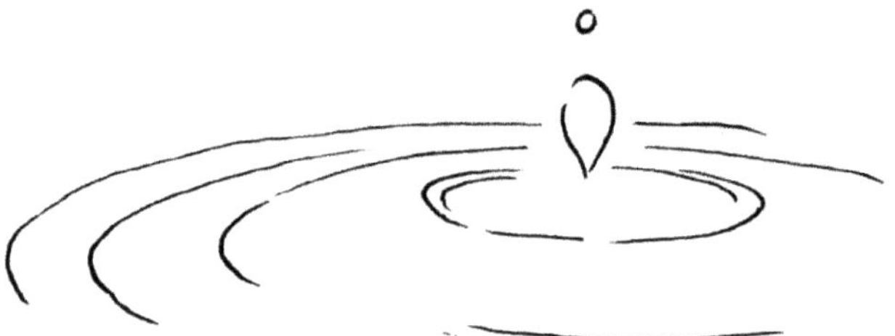

I don't get butterflies anymore
I get bumblebees
Knowing later it will sting
I get seasick
Waves of regret a familiar ring
I get stage fright
You stole my desire to sing.

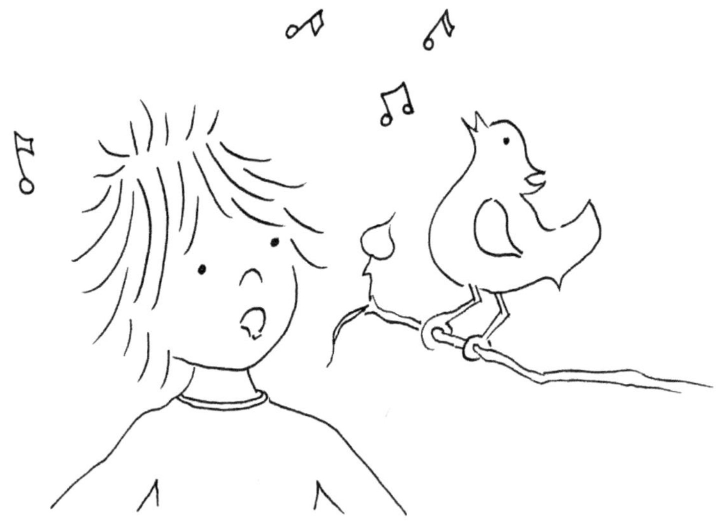

I am a woman
Until you decide I'm a painting
An exhibit for your entertaining
You observe but do not understand

I am a woman
Until you decide I'm an armrest
That unless your needs are being met
I take up too much space

I am a woman
Until you decide I'm a souvenir
To show you've reached a new frontier
You collect stories and leave behind hearts

I am more than a woman
But I will never be enough for you.

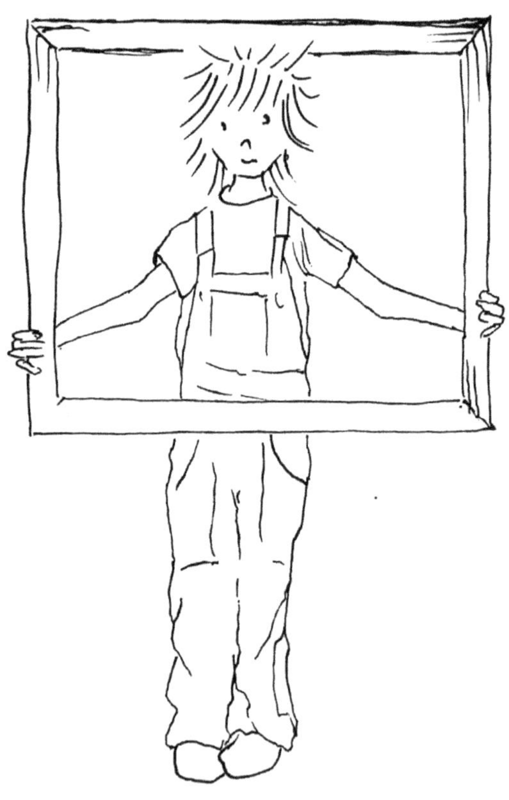

I'm painted a shade of red with your eyes
Becoming a one-dimensional object
In your monochromatic museum

I wait for your gaze to find me uninteresting

My soul is carved by your knife-like words
I am an empty jack-o-lantern
For the haunted house in your head

But the only person you've scared is me.

I learned to lower my eyes
Because making eye contact is their invitation

I learned to say I have a boyfriend
Because "no" is never enough

I learned where to cross the street
And when to put on my sunglasses

I learned to walk quicker
Smile smaller
Talk quieter

But I haven't learned enough.

I used to trustfall into anyone's hands
Never doubted intentions or plans
Until you let me slip through your fingers like sand
Now even my gut can't be trusted
To tell me something I'll understand.

I hold my story
Like one holds blades of grass
In a wide open field
Only for a second
I let memories pass through my fingers
I let moments of pain be gathered by others
I let passersby skip through my joy
Like you hold my cheek
Only for an instant
I hold my story with an open hand
Hoping you will want to hold it too.

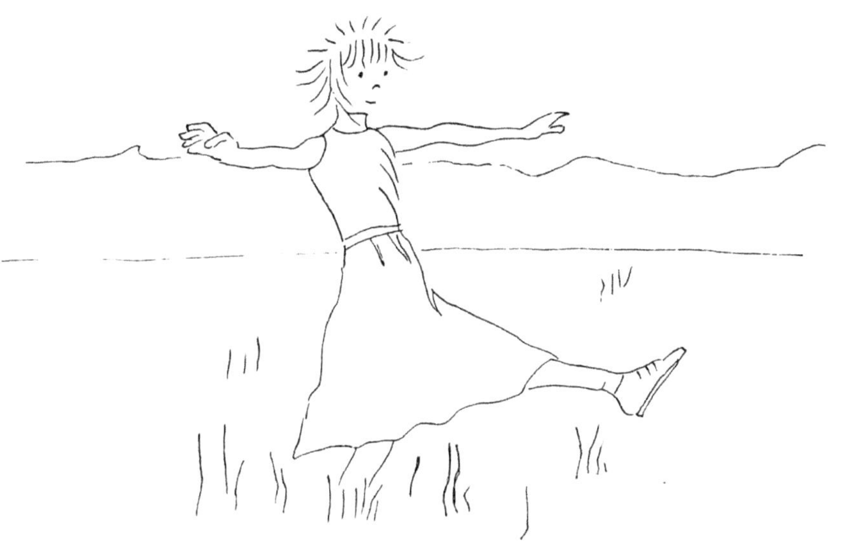

"You have given a lot of yourself"

And into my lap fell the memories
Of stories I told before knowing the ending
Of dances I performed before learning the steps
I offered bouquets
Made up of every dream and doubt
Even with petals falling
Even with buds unopened
I offered all my heart
To strangers who couldn't hold it

I didn't understand they only wanted fractions
They didn't understand I can only give wholes.

Is there a word
For an event that is a beginning and an end
Maybe it's sunset

Is there a word
For a moment that bears joy and loneliness
Maybe it's memory

Is there a word
For a longing to be closer and further away
Maybe it's your name.

My sadness comes packaged in many hues

Navy blue ballads
From a crimson red heart
Baby blue tears
On rosy red cheeks
Laments in blue ink
And verses whispered soft pink

Melancholy is a murky stew
Heartache is more than just blue.

If you only want me in pieces
I'd rather you leave aside my heart

Don't ask me for a smile
When I can fill a song with laughter
Stop searching for a trail of petals
When you see me plant a bitter garden

You asked for pieces of my heart
But I will only give all of me.

I save a seat for grief
In the gardens of my dreams
And in the margins of my stories

I save a seat for grief
In the breaths between words
In the pages between poems
In the silence between steps

For if there is strength in weakness
Surely there is goodness
And grace
And gold
In grief.

Let me be soft

Let me swim in my emotions
They are as deep as the ocean
But I am pulled by the tides

Anger is a forward motion
Love is an explosion
Joy is my devotion
Together they could drown me

But my soul has danced in these storms before
And my spirit knows the nearness of shore
So I embrace the weather that carries me
To the Savior that can calm the seas.

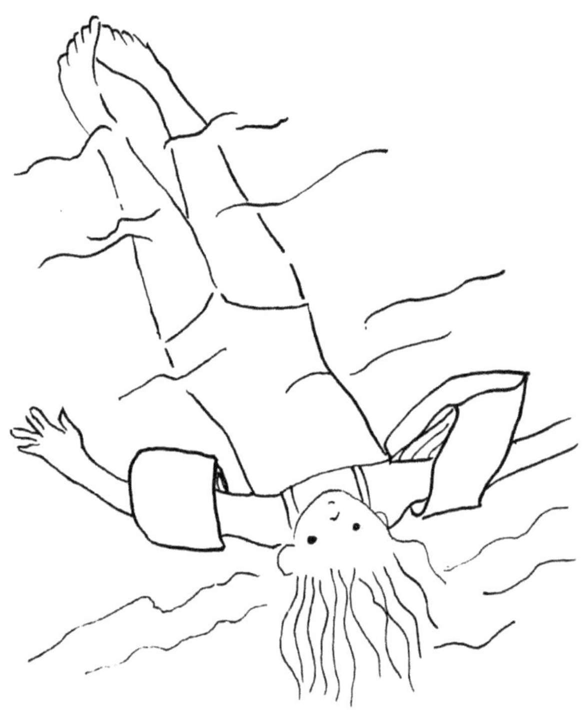

I can't hold on to anything
Can't hold a note long enough to sing
Can't hold my breath long enough to swim

Nothing stays
But One Day
The old will pass away

The letting go will meet the letting in
And sand slipping through my fingers
Will become a castle on the beach

I will welcome waves that ebb and flow
I will find comfort in what cannot be grasped
I will find joy knowing this too shall pass.

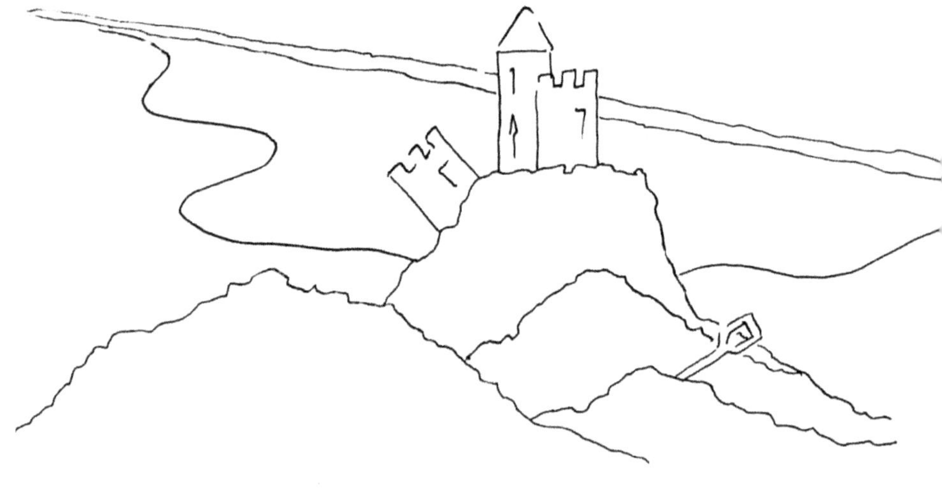

I long for rain
That refreshes
Restores

Rain that rinses
Yesterday's sidewalk chalk

Rain that rejuvenates
Rain reveals
The beauty lying beneath dirt
As it makes way
For bouquets to blossom.

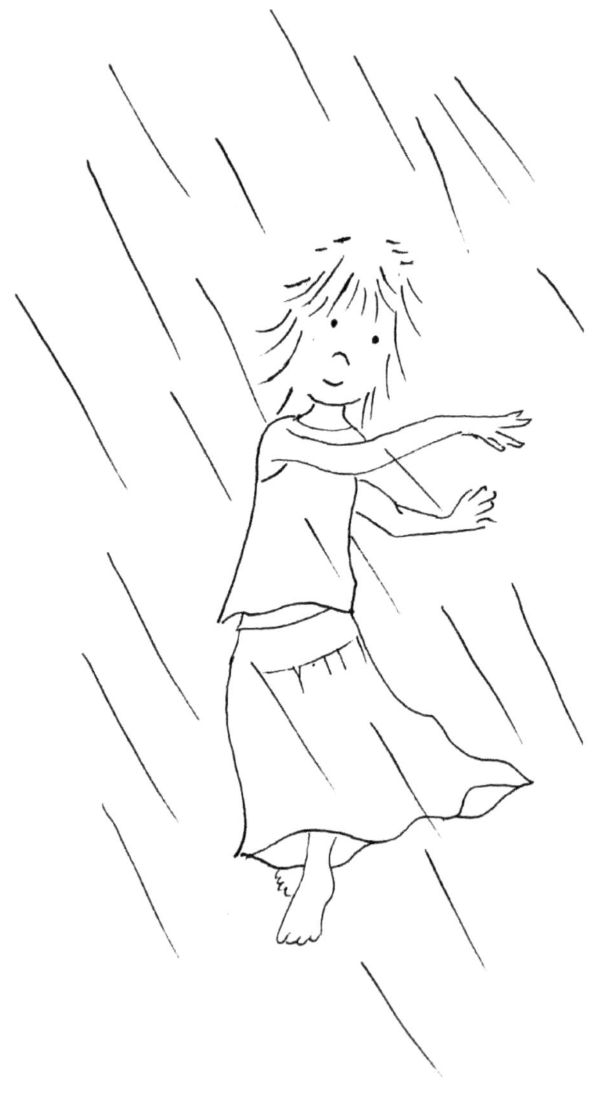

I wonder where I'm going

Led by a heart
Lost in emotion
A compass that's easily swayed

Led by a head
Loaded by voices
That disagree on the destination ahead.

You knit me together in my mother's womb
And yet I wonder
If You used the right type of yarn
And yet I doubt
That You never lost a stitch
And still I ponder
If You followed a pattern

You knit me together in my mother's womb
And still I question my worth.

If only
We could share our thoughts through the clouds
I would send happy memories
On cotton candy pink
I would tell bedtime stories
Against golden backdrops
Wish you would get well soon
On a raincloud
Whisper words of wonder
On light and airy veils
If only
We could share our thoughts through the clouds
You would think of me every time you look up.

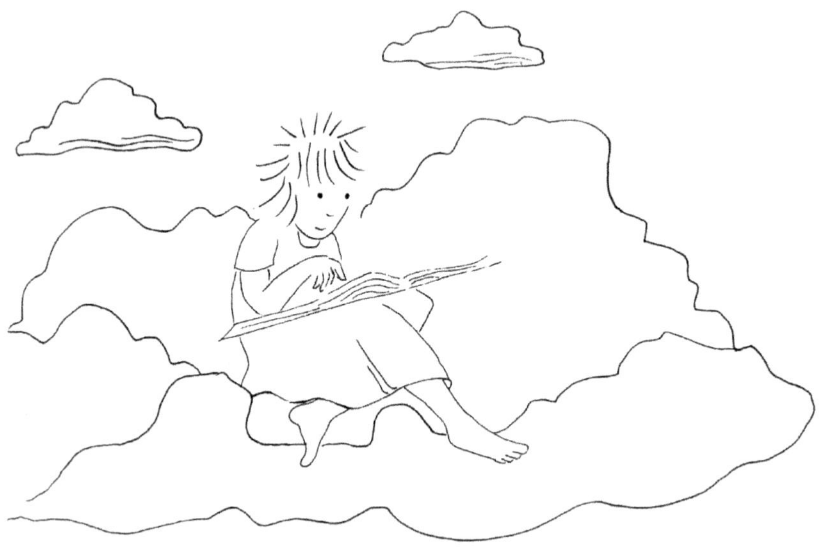

I mourned the loss
Of what was never mine

When I was given rainclouds
Though I had planned for sunshine

When I read the tragic end
Not the closure in my mind

When my bucket stayed empty
There were no shells left to find

I cling to hope like the string on a balloon
Believing dreams always come true with time
I miss your company
But it was never mine.

I will dance under any sky
But just once
I'd like to dance in your light

I will listen to any song
But how I long
For my name to be your lyrics

I will marvel at every flower
But how I wish
They were from you.

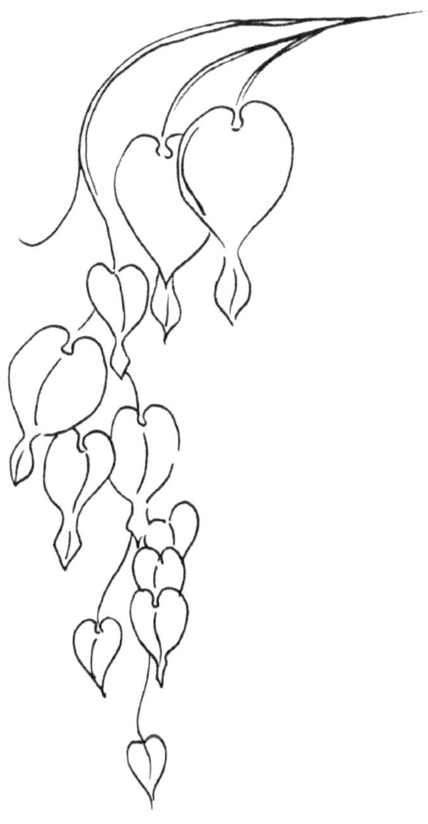

In bold black ink
I write about my pain
Words so heavy they sink
To the bedrock of my gut
Until miraculously
The graves turn into gardens
The bones into coral reefs
My body into a home
Built by rhymes as sweet as honeycomb.

He was summer
I melted under his rays
But when summer became fall
Only memories remained
Of happy days

I was spring
I sang the songs of robins
When all too soon they flew away
The nest that was a home
Became a coffin.

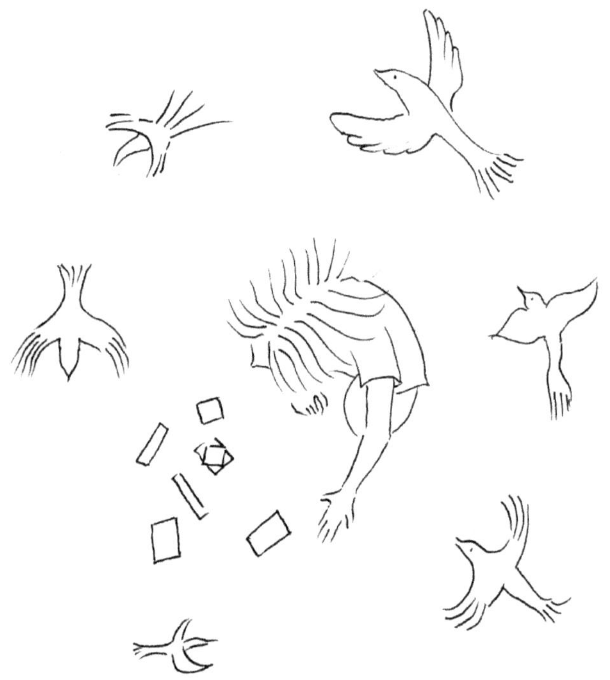

The names before yours
I once pronounced with a melody
Are now so thick with memory
They get caught in my throat

Will the wind blow them away
As though written in dust
Will the marks where I carved each letter
Leave a scar
Will the rain erase the faces
From the poems I cried

I wonder about the songs before ours
About the photographs
The footprints
The futures
Before ours

Will I ever forget
My past before you.

French people say *bon courage*
Or *good courage*
Instead of good luck
How much more strength in a wish

French people say *tu me manques*
Or *you are missing from me*
Not I miss you
How much more emptiness in a memory

French people say *magnifique* instead of pretty
And *adore* instead of love
They say *bisous* instead of see you
And *adieu* instead of goodbye
When it's the last goodbye

How much more tragic a departure in French.

"Play me the song that broke you"

Waves crash onto the shore disrupting the night
Hands search for a heart and find the stars
Bodies look for a home and find the sand

I have heard fingers kiss harp strings
Trees become coffins
But the sound of your heart crumbling
Was the song that broke me.

Ortolan
You flew within reach of my hands
Long enough for your wings to know my thumb
Long enough for your song to catch my breath
But not long enough
Ortolan
You flew within reach of my hands
Before I learned how to say goodbye.

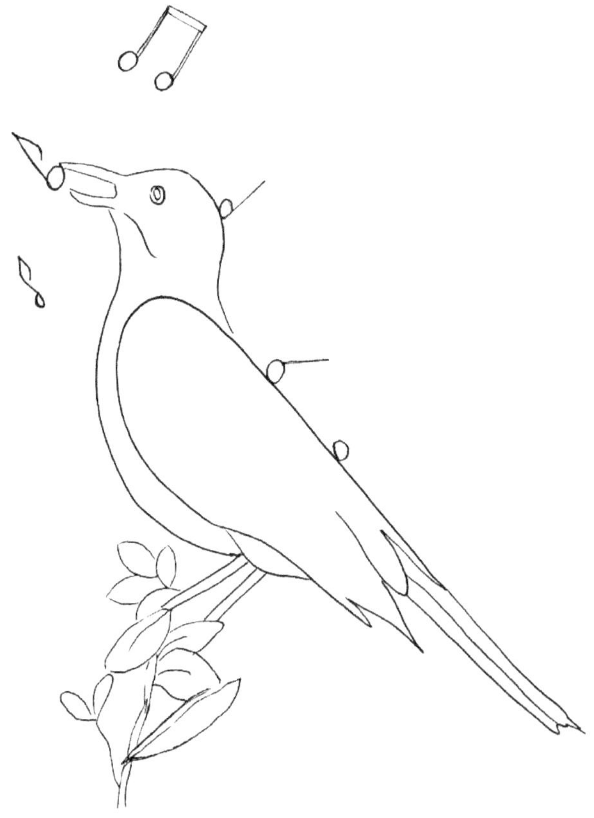

The world seems so small
When a city becomes your neighbourhood
When passersby are faces you know
When a familiar scent is on someone new
But my world grew so much bigger
When I met you.

I reach for a hand across the ocean
My body a bridge
Stretched so thin
It won't hold the weight of memories

I can't hold on

But to let go
Would erase the lines of poetry
You carved into my hand
To accept that my fingerprint
Lost the ripple of your name

I can't let go.

There are days where the clouds hang heavier
And the mourning doves lament louder

Still You are there.

Nights where darkness whispers wordlessly
And the wind sighs stoically

Still You are there.

If You are in a silent grave
A lion's den
A mother's womb

Surely You're in my darkness too.

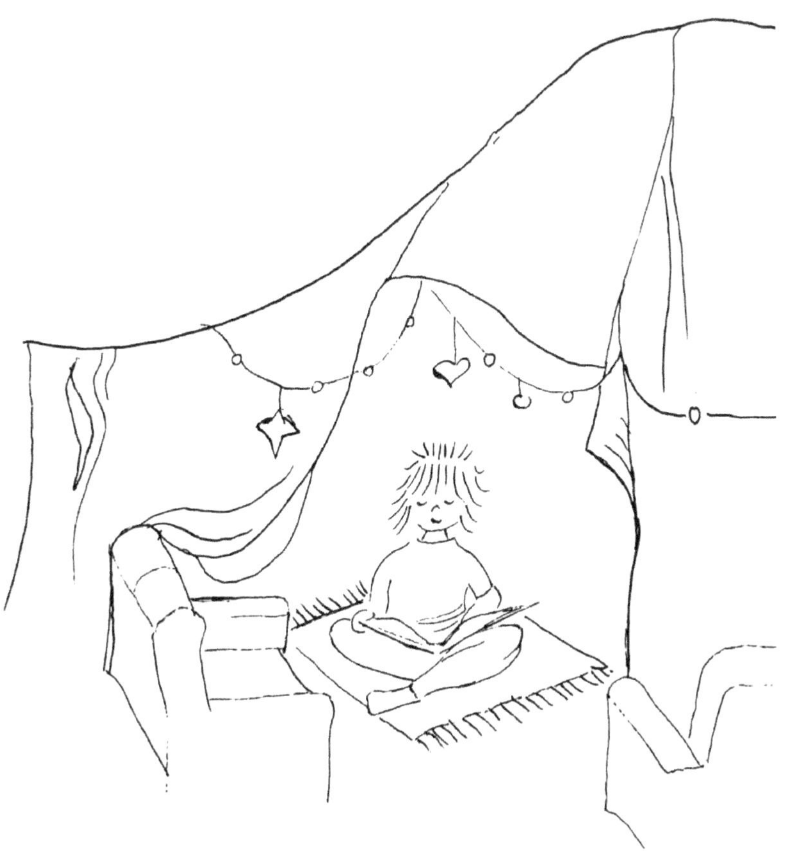

Sometimes I wish I could bottle up
How it feels to be lonely
The heaviness that presses on my heart
As I dare it to beat
The emptiness that greets my hand
As I reach for a star

I want to bottle up this feeling
Because one day
When my heart beats for more than just me
When my hand meets the warmth of your soul
I will only be able to remember
How it feels to be loved.

All we wanted was time
An abundance like rainfall
Rather than the lonely drops
That didn't quench our thirst

We couldn't stretch them any thinner
The minutes
The moments
The drops
When all we wanted was time.

I am waiting
For minutes that feel like sunshine
For days that feel like summer
For weeks that feel like Sundays

I am waiting
For nights that look like sleepovers
For afternoons that look like storybooks
For mornings that look like surprises

I am waiting for a lifetime
That reminds me of salvation
In newness, in joy and in grace.

I have witnessed
A love so beautiful
So simple
So complete
A love that dances to jazz
A love that radiates joy
A love so bountiful
I am satisfied
To just be a witness.

I'm not one to forget sunsets

The colours may melt together
And the shapes of clouds blur forever
But I won't forget
How our songs were pink and orange harmonies
How our stories were carried on seagull wings
How our laughter echoed against the first stars

I will always cherish
The sunsets we painted.

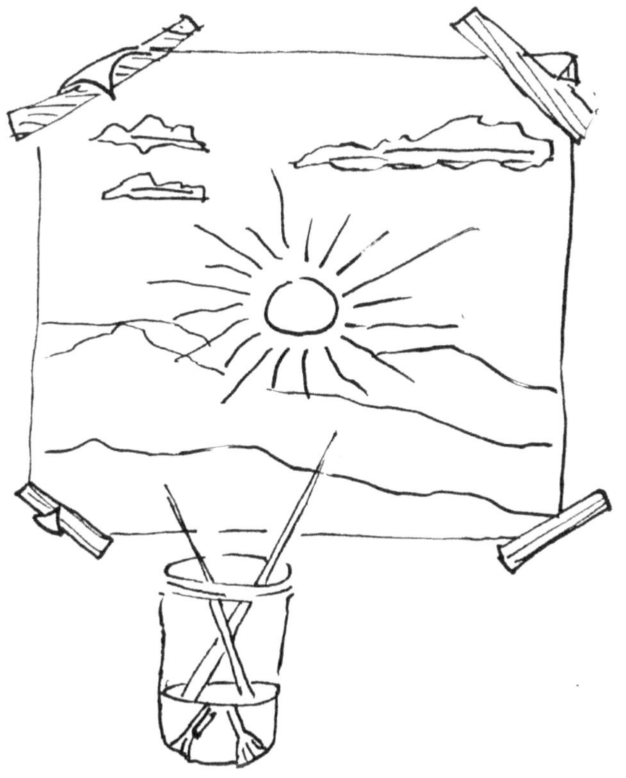

When summer ended
The sun set so suddenly
I was left with shrivelled skin
Wishing I could still smell the sea
When summer ended
Fall came with a new palette
Asters and golden rods growing from graves
Every field a canvas of purple and yellow
I saw new constellations
Join hands with new songs
Though summer ended
His abundance was endless.

To be single in the city of love
Is to notice tenderness
Decorating every street corner
From flower shops to wine spots
I notice it too
In people walking home with baguettes for two
In museums asking to be explored in conversation

To be single in the city of love
Is to have an extra chair at the Café de Flore
To have a little more sidewalk space on the Seine
And yet
It is to daydream carelessly in quiet bookstores
To wander aimlessly in unknown quartiers
And to delight endlessly in people-watching cafés.

I got lost trying to find myself
I searched for bearings on a broken compass
Traced my steps on faded footprints
I lost myself
Then I found You

I found Your breath within me
As I danced with fading strength
Your voice answering my silence
As I stood in awe amongst the clouds
Your arms rocking me gently
As I was tossed by rolling waves

I was always found by You.

Loneliness is an oversized sweater
I wear it until it feels as homey as my skin
I find comfort in the threadbare fabric
Until the weight that was a blanket
Becomes a burden
And I want nothing more than to wear a sundress
To embrace the warmth of presence on my face

But when winds of solitude feel closer than the sun
I will not run from what is near
For in loneliness I find peace
In solitude my hope will increase.

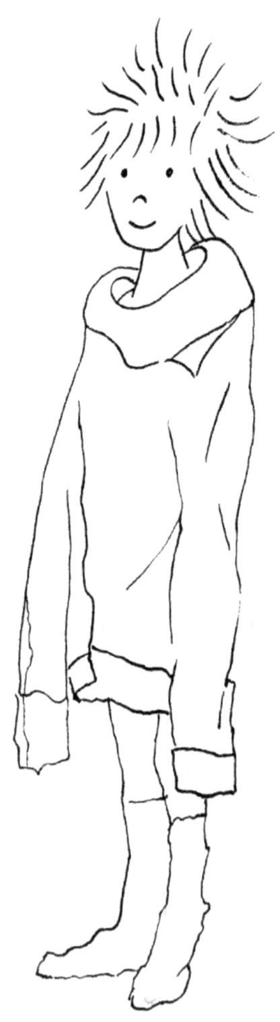

I have found
Faith sprouting
From silent seconds when coffee drips
From a slow setting sun on empty evenings
From patient prayers yielding blurry answers
I have found
Faith growing
In silence
Emptiness
Patience
In the sacred space
Between lull and longing.

Love Has a Home

Morning waited
    faithfully
For me to draw back the curtains
    gratefully
Then took up every corner
Like honey fills a jar
Light has made a home in me

Then robins came and filled my nest
Made the bed so I could rest
Exchanged empty echoes for melodies
And gave me space for elegies
Love has made a home in me

I will not be defined by my pain
But I will be defined by the healing
For the One who hears the broken-hearted
Has made a home in me.

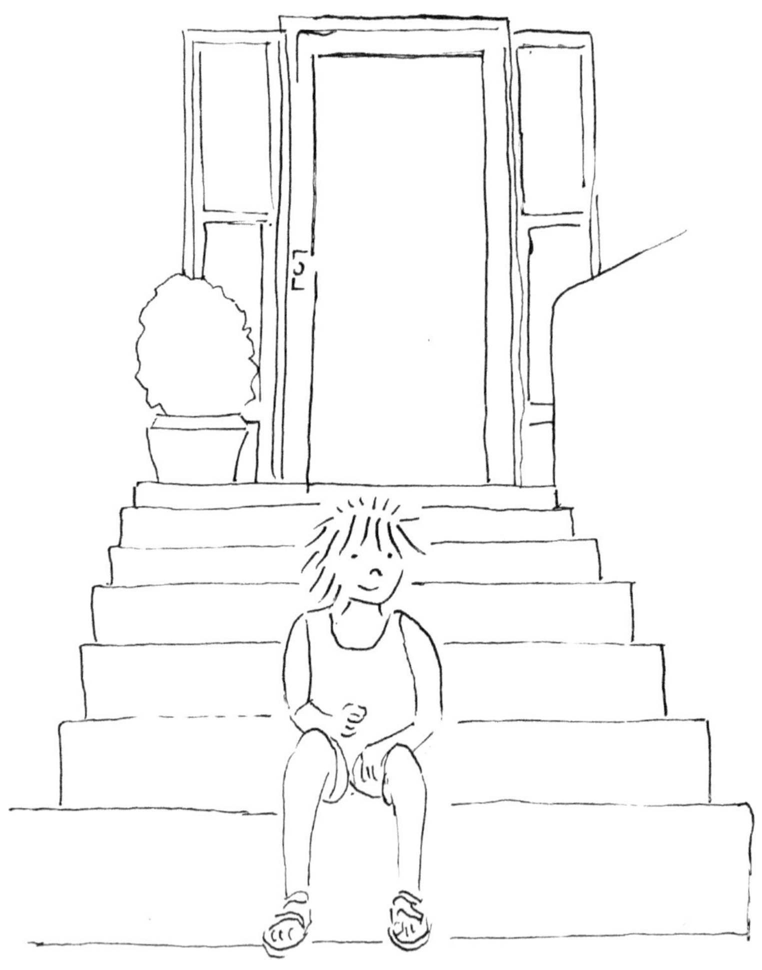

For now
I'm here

There will be worries and failures another day
Messy rooms and busy heads another day
Loneliness and longing another day
Scattered memories and missing pieces another day
Unswept triggers and mixed-up names another day

But for now
I'm here.

There can be empty landscapes
The space between two seasons
The shade between two colours
And there can be joy

There can be quiet mornings
The pause before a piano awakens
The prayers before two hands unite
And there can be joy

There can be music boxes without melodies
And vases without flowers
And hearts without a beloved
And still there can be joy.

I've never known what it feels like to be in love
Only what it feels like to wonder

Yet how wonderful it is to know
There are still feelings to be felt
Like how the air feels on Mount Everest
How a surfer feels riding a wave
And how home feels with a person

There are still colours to be seen
How vibrant the ocean's floor
How orange a Hawaiian evening
And how inimitable the light in your eyes

There are still songs to be sung
Melodies to compose
And artists to inspire

Still bouquets to behold
Dishes to delight in
And dance partners to discover

I hope this life is always filled
With wonder.

Alone at a table meant for two
I welcome the company
Of a pigeon
Or a chickadee
For they remind me
How much presence is in the small body of a bird
Like the presence of wind that moves silent trees
Like the presence of raindrops that composes a song
They remind me
Of how He fills the quiet corners of my life
And resides in the closest quarters of my heart
For the empty seat at a table meant for two
Is never really empty
Is it?

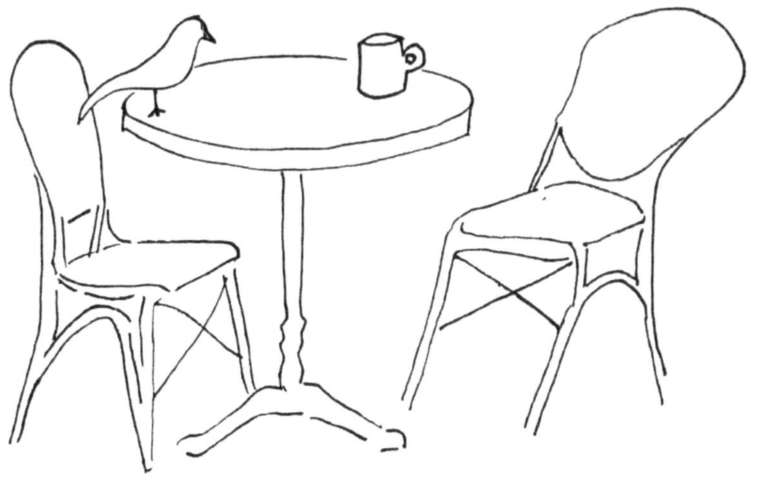

All this time
I've been standing in foyers
Approaching as a guest
Waiting for an invitation

When all this time
I've had a seat at His table
The door left unlocked
Garden planted for me

I am my Saviour's daughter
This is my home.

I have arrived
At a place without horizons
Where my feet feel firmly planted
Where my hands feel fully free

I have arrived
At spring's open gates
Every morning full of wonder
Every breath wholly new

I have arrived
At the ocean's breathless joy
Waves of perfect peace
Currents of pure poetry

One day you'll open your eyes
And find you're here too.

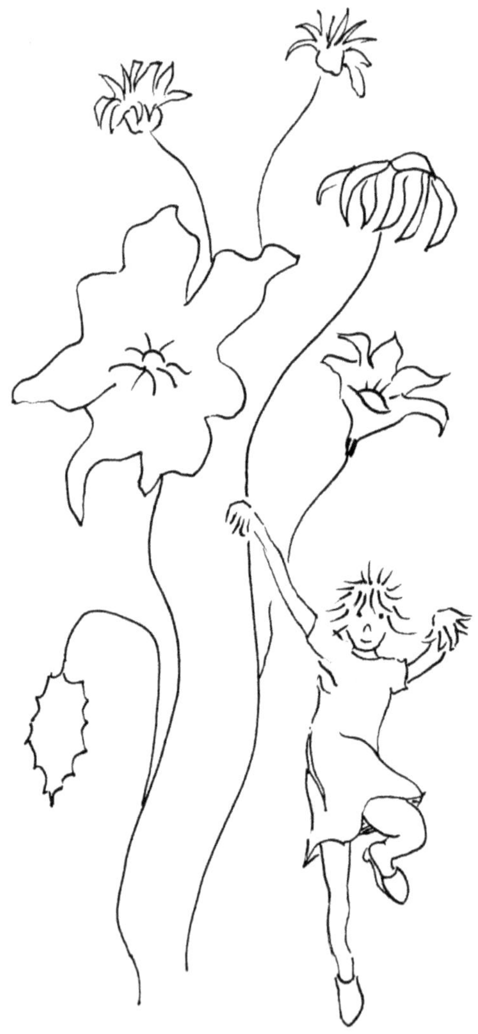

You will find your way
    as a vase forms out of clay
    as an arc grows from rays and rain
Beauty will show the way
And you will find your place
    as a heart clings to a face
    as a hand sees stars to trace
Love will make a way
    and you will let it stay.

I looked for healing in the wind
For lost leaves of last season to drift away
For gusts of refreshment to bring restoration
But healing was not in the wind

I looked for healing in the earthquake
For the bones of my weary home to fall
For a new landscape to grow from fresh ground
But healing was not in the earthquake

I looked for healing in the fire
For weighty debris to melt away
For refining flames to reveal true gold
But healing was not in the fire

And after the wind, the earthquake and the fire
I heard the sound of my Saviour's gentle whisper
A voice calling me daughter
A voice calling me home
And I found healing.

On the horizon there will be days
You will feel the sun's arms embracing your own
And you won't have to look down to know
He has clothed you in gold

Evermore there will be days
You will find your laughter meeting the hills
Though you won't hear an echo you'll know
He has joined in your song.

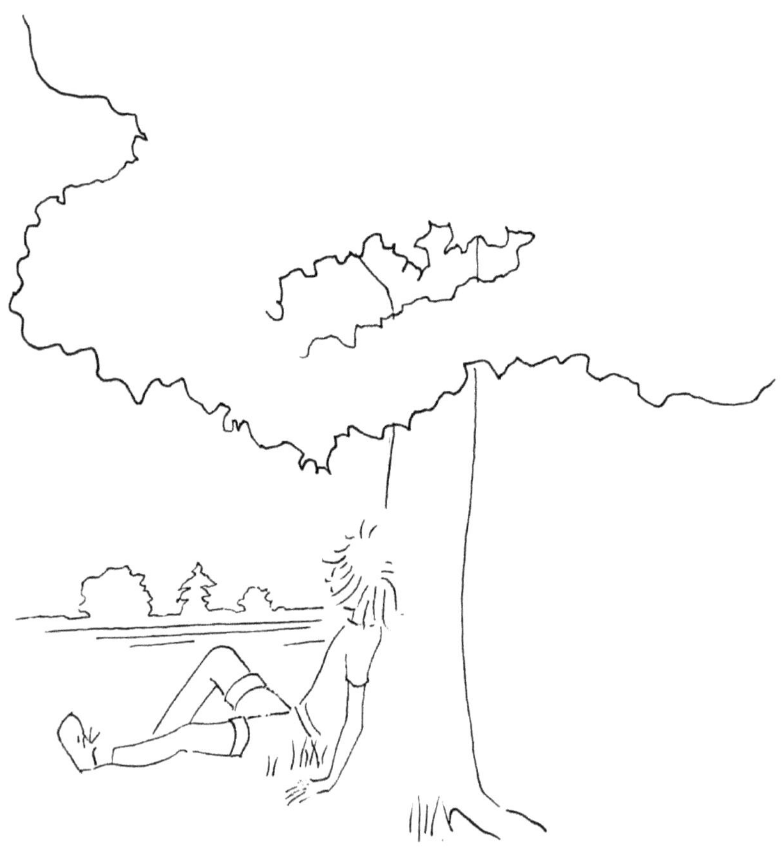

How do you befriend the ocean
If not by embracing the wind
If not by laughing at the waves
Waves of grace
Waves of glory
Wave after wave
Peace belongs to me
Like the horizon belongs to my eyes
Like the sand belongs to my feet
I walk on stones older than love
I breathe in light new as the day
Oh Sunday of serenity.

Tell me again
That singleness is loneliness
And I will tell you
How I woke up to the sun wishing me good morning
Presence filled every corner of my room
Peace filled every inch of my being
How can loneliness reside
Where there is fullness?

Even on dark days I have company
The constant sound of raindrops
A soothing metronome
I listen to them instead of the silence
How can loneliness reside
Where there is contentment?

So I won't wish upon a star
That I may be where you are
And I won't ask if you are far
For what is distance to a star
And what is darkness
To one who walks in light.

I've stopped looking for *the one*
As if a single person completes me
For my purpose lies not in a sum
Happiness isn't equal to me plus you
I refuse to crown another my sun
When light has always shone in me.

But I will welcome one
Who's hungry for soul food
Who feasts on gratitude
And gelato in magnitude
Who slow dances with joy
Knowing life is enjoyed
In overalls and corduroy.

You are a new day
Your resilience is the monarch's soft flight
Your courage is the morning's first song
Your joy is the faintest dew

One day you'll realize you don't miss him
One day you'll sing a love song to yourself
One day you'll hear the echo of your voice

One day you'll know you are not the same
You are a new day.

I knew I was home
When arrivals were anticipated
Knowing she would come with ice cream and stories

I knew I was home
When rituals were rose-coloured
Saturday morning markets
Sunday evening strolls

I knew I was home
When I claimed laidback landmarks
A taco stand
A coffee shop
A reading spot

When friends of friends became friends of mine
And I was content to stay inside
I knew I was home.

I am finding
A voice that holds a symphony
I am becoming
A woman dressed in freedom
I am learning
To inhale softness like a melody.

Finally
I am finding language to tell my story
Planted in the silence of untraveled mornings
Growing in the softness of well-disguised wounds
Buried in the embrace of delicate nights.

My fingers are the first to dance
A waltz with the wind
Before my ears hear a melody
Before my feet discover a tune

My thumbs caress the softest cheeks
Rocks made smooth by the waves
Leaves made silver by the rain

I cross a flowery field
Holding May's hand
Her laughter is a chorus of chickadees
Her arm is a hawthorn branch

In the sand I write a love poem to spring
Her tears of joy carry my words with the waves
Nothing remains
But my open hands.

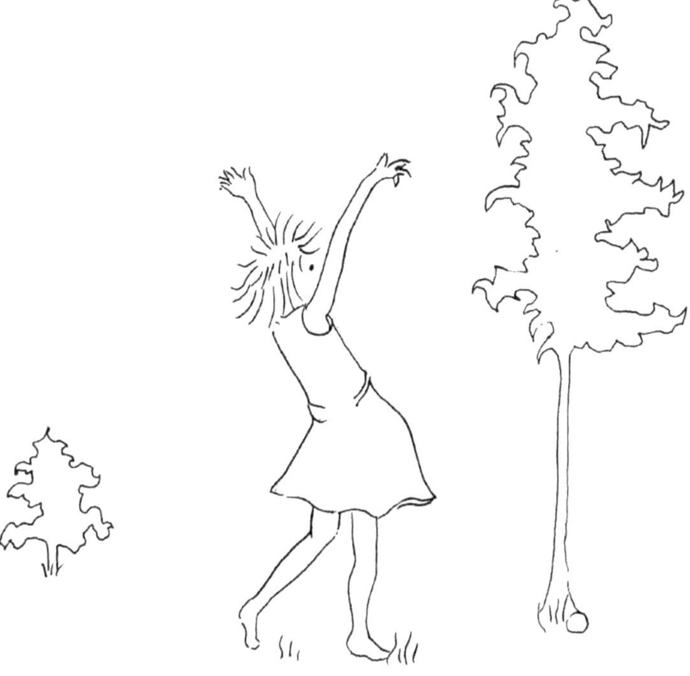

Let the shade of a tree on a hot day remind you
You are loved

Let the wind that plays with your hair assure you
You are loved

Listen to the birds as they sing to you
You are loved

Give the stars permission to reveal to you
You are loved

Let every breath you release to the world thank God
That you are loved.

Even more than I'm grateful for colourful skies
I'm grateful my eyes are instruments
That love to harmonize
With my heart and my head
They are synchronized
Thus a view I've seen a thousand times
Still carries joy
As softly as wind chimes.

Take me to paradise
Where clouds kiss the mountains
Orange roofs complement sunset skies
And grassy meadows fall and rise.

Drive with me
Down endless winding roads
As the moon begins to glow
And hearts continue to grow
Watered by music from long ago
Happiness overflows.

I can't explain
How it bubbles up
Warms me from my core
Refreshes me like peppermint tea

It doesn't make sense
How securely it settles
How deeply it extends
Grounded as an oak tree

I can't fathom how far Your love reaches
To galaxies even telescopes can't see
I will never understand
How You hold the heavens
And still delight in me.

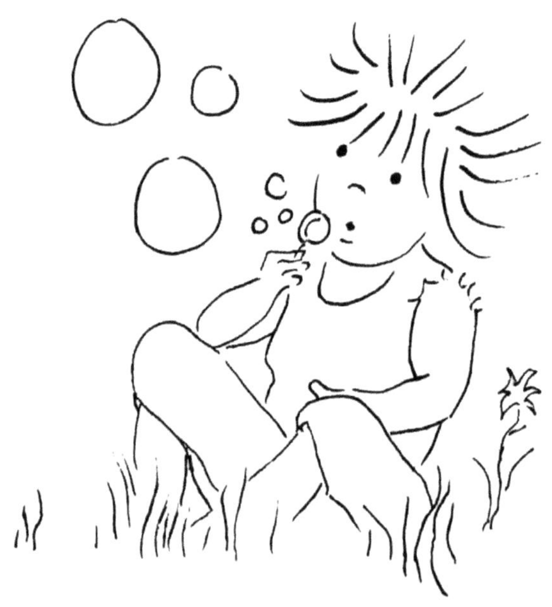

You are not incomplete
Not a half to a whole
Not missing a piece

Together the sun and the rain make a rainbow
But the sun on its own fills the whole earth with light
And the rain by itself allows the growth of new life

As a field bursting with every bright shade
As a painting that bears the artist's name
As a song from a harp brings perfect peace

You are complete.

Passion tastes like Indian food
She burns my tongue
And still leaves me wanting more
I go back for seconds and thirds

A cacophony fills me from the inside out
It's not in tune to the melody I'm used to
But still I choose
To recognize the music

We all bring unique offerings to this potluck
And together create a symphony so delightful
We could never again consume bread and butter
Or settle for last night's leftovers

We crave the creation of new harmonies
Orchestrated by a common desire for change
Satisfaction meets my lips for only a moment
Always hungry for more.

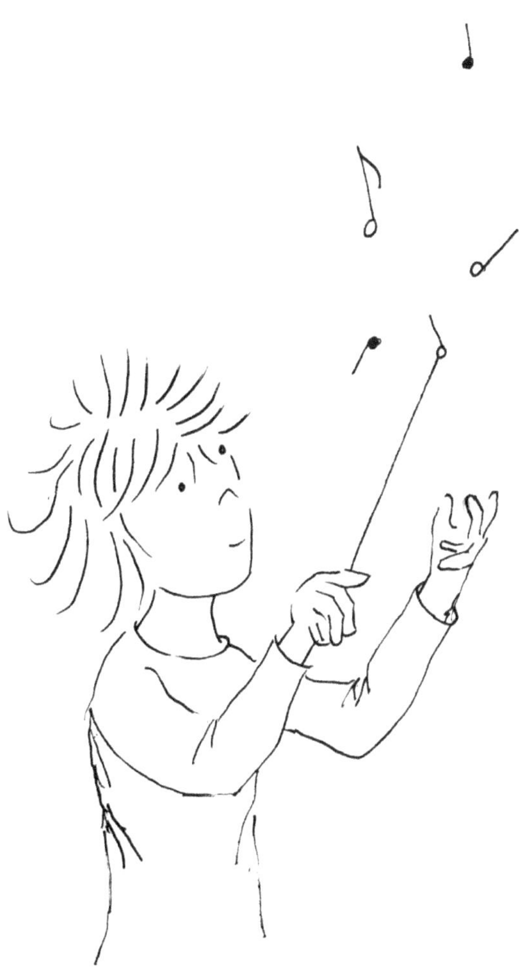

In deserts
Of questions unexplained
And expectations unfulfilled
Your love
Is an anthem like rain

You breathe
Words into my veins
That I write into verses

Only you
Can carefully take my pain
And transform it into poetry.

Dawn breaks
Goodness rises like dew
Every morning
Your mercies are new
Palms open
I reap what You sow
In fields of plenty
My basket overflows

Each wild strawberry
A vibrant witness
Each delicate daisy
Brings me to stillness
Breathless wonder
In every bouquet
Gifts of grace
In every day.

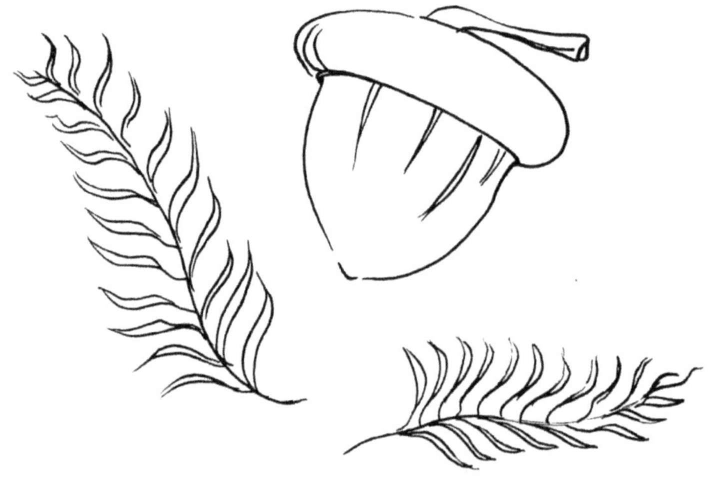

If I've ever been in love
It was when
The mountains met pastel pink clouds
My heart met Yours
And the air was so crisp it crackled
Surely
It was made for me

When ocean and sand became a boundless border
Your arms embraced mine
And I discovered how it feels to be weightless
Surely
It was made for me

When darkness softly bled onto grassy pillows
Your stars kissed me goodnight
And wonder reached beyond all explanation
Surely
It was made for me.

I knew a heart made cold from eternal winters
And now I know
A shoulder that lets the sun soak through
A hand that accepts offerings of love
A face that waits for colour to bleed
Now I know
A dancer who lives for spring.

The miracle of a changing sky dawned on me
As I flew beneath a pink canopy
That spilt across the heavens
I've never seen that exact shade before

This is what liberty feels like

A little later
The sun began her exodus
Opal clouds formed a mosaic
And an artist lined every gap with gold

This is what harmony feels like.

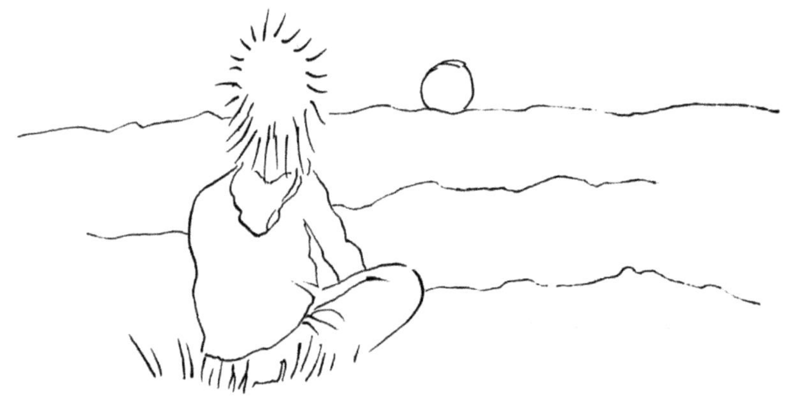

I love when baguettes are in backpacks
And eclairs are for breakfast

I love seeing old men in berets
And old buildings in sunshine

I love hearing couples speak in poetry
And tourists sing "La vie en rose"

In Paris
Love is never far away.

There are people who feel like summer
Endlessly warm
Whose presence is quiet and consistent
Like the chirping of crickets
And in the dreadful darkness of wasted worries
Their little lights like fireflies
Are all the warmth you need.

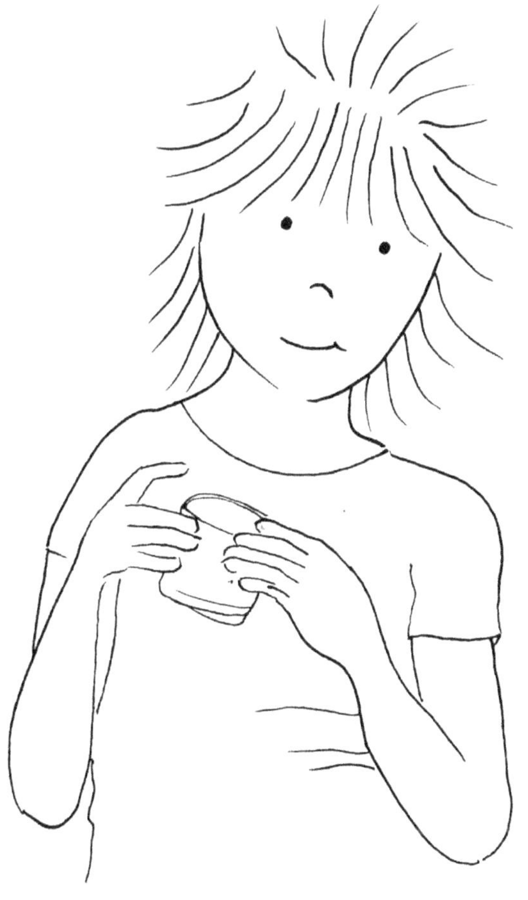

The best of friends will appreciate
What you've never noticed about yourself
The expression that became a catchphrase
The endearing way you wave goodbye
And the extra time you take to tell stories

They will tell you how strangers react to your smile
What makes your sense of fashion unique
And how they recognized your laugh
From across a room

What a gift it is
To see myself through their eyes.

Winds and rivers
You refresh my soul

I swim in currents of summer air
Floating on a breeze
That lifts my heart to the heavens
I fly on the backs of rolling waves
Soaring on a stream that knows the way north

Winds and rivers
You carry me home.

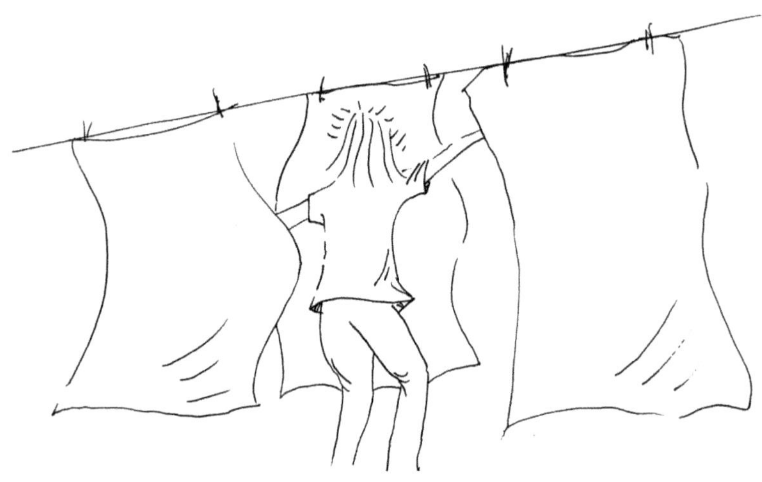

Now I see
No love compares
To the Father's heart for me
No song as melodious
As the promises whispered to me
No breath more grounded
Than the peace He plants in me
No joy more complete
Than dancing in His presence

Now I know
May I know evermore.

I planted little seeds of joy
And watered them with hope

I saw sunflowers grow
From surprise sunsets with quiet company
Roses blossomed
From restful reading dates in the park
Daisies sprouted
From delightful days in curious museums
Violets unfolded
From velvety coffee at the Vietnamese café

I planted little seeds of joy
And woke up to a garden.

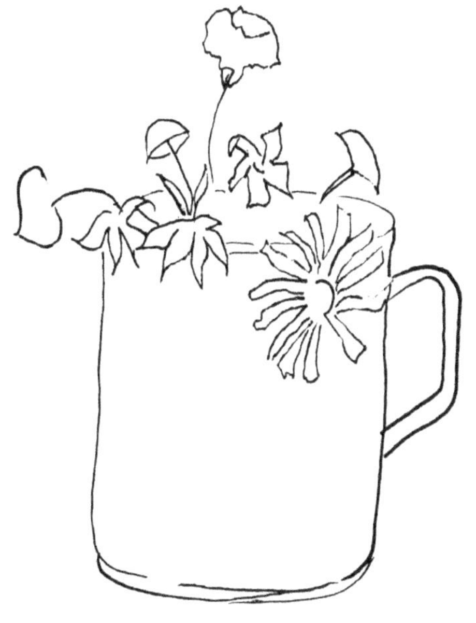

I will let my joy be seen

I will laugh off-key
Sing out of tune
And dance out of line

I will dress too brightly
Smile too widely
And react too largely

I will live as though I'm never too much
I will let people enjoy my joy.

A 99-year-old man once told me:
"Tu as toute une vie devant toi"

I pondered what makes up *a whole life*
And thought maybe it's tangos

The slow ones that take us
From graceful on our feet
To grateful in our hearts
That such a time
A partner
A night in front of the opera
Exists

With every step
I take a breath
Of my life that is just beginning
As he takes a breath among his last
Yet 21 and 99 seem much closer
When life is just a moment
A breath
A tango.

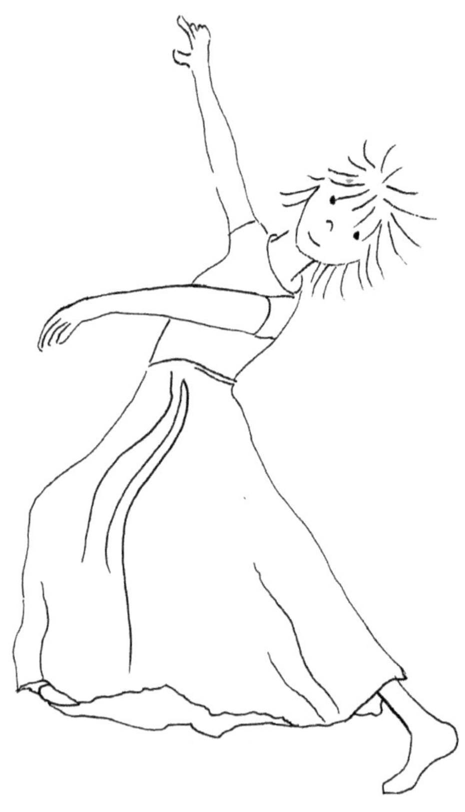

May you never approach an open field
    without the sudden urge to skip

May you never run to the ocean
    and stifle the wave of laughter that hits

May you never cease to find joy
    from glimpsing a sunset

May you never hide the tears that come
    from the view on top of a mountain

May you never resist opening
    your arms to a windy day

May you feel deeply
Live widely
And love abundantly.

Sometimes I forget
How good joy tastes
Until suddenly
Music is echoing on every skyscraper
And strangers are asking "may we have this dance"
A man is playing the harmonica
Another is blowing bubbles
And a little girl is moving like she's in her living room
I close my eyes
And I'm in my living room
I can't believe I get to live
With this much joy.

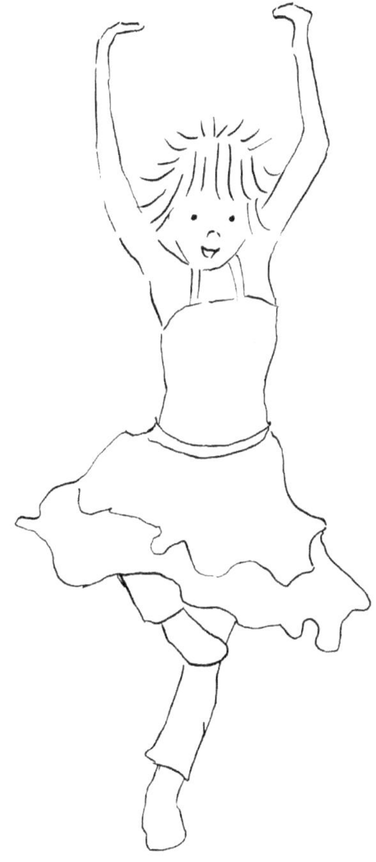

NOTES

The poem on page 5 is inspired by Michel Pleau's *J'aurai bientôt ton âge*, specifically the following verses: "longtemps // j'ai oublié les mains de mon enfance".

The poem on page 7 is inspired by the following verses, performed by Pierre Morency on *La Nuit de la Poésie* in 1970: "je n'étais pas un enfant // j'étais une bombe".

A line from page 9 was inspired by the following words of Jean-Noël Pontbriand: "un peu d'amour suspendu au grenier de l'enfance".

I was inspired by the following Charles Spurgeon quote for the poem on page 50: "I have learned to kiss the wave that throws me against the Rock of Ages".

The poem on page 57 begins with a portion of the following verse from the NIV Bible, "For you created my inmost being; you knit me together in my mother's womb" Psalm 139:13.

ACKNOWLEDGEMENTS

I am indebted to so many people who encouraged me to write and share my poetry.

Lizzy, I've tried so many times to write you a poem, but your friendship means more to me than words can do justice. Thank you for being my biggest fan.

To Leah, Aleeze and Sarah, whose support was so tangible. Thank you for your confidence in me, and for all the ways you invested in this process.

To Julia, Prachi, Oda, Munju, Ariane, Agnella, Alice, Grégoire and Christina, who were among the first to know that I was writing this book. Thank you for matching my excitement more than I could have hoped for.

To every person who sent or spoke a word of encouragement. I valued them all.

To my friends at Mill Stream Bible Camp and Power to Change York who gave me opportunities to share my writing. Thank you for seeing the best in me.

To my teachers, notably Ms Ellis and Swann
Paradis, who ignited a spark for writing.

To my family at C3 Toronto, C3 Paris, Pathway
Church and Living Hope, who were invested in my
growth. Christ's love is tangible because of you.

To my thoughtful editor, Rachel Huckel. Thank you
for your dedication to my work and your belief in
me as a writer.

To my siblings, Elliott, Egan and Elsa. I am so proud
to be your sister. Thank you for keeping me
humble and supporting me so strongly.

To my siblings in heaven, Travis, Noah and
Mitchell. I have faith because of you.

To Mom and Dad, for letting me pursue every
dream. Before I was born you believed I would be a
light, and then you gave me every opportunity to
shine. Thank you.

And to Jesus. I could write of your love forever.

ABOUT THE AUTHOR

Eleana Norton is an education student at Glendon College and a French teacher. She is an appreciator of the arts, frequents local cafés, attends cheap concerts, and reads often. She grew up in Peterborough, Ontario but loves to call Toronto her home. *Little Dancers* is her first poetry collection.

You can find her work on Instagram @eleana.poetry.

You are welcome to write to her at eleana.poetry@gmail.com.